CLAN
STEWART

Extensively Revised

COMPILED BY
Alan McNie

CASCADE PUBLISHING COMPANY
Scotland

Genealogical Research:
Research regrettably cannot be undertaken by the publisher. A
non-profit organisation, The Scots Ancestry Research Society,
3 Albany Street, Edinburgh, undertake research for an agreed fee.

ISBN 0 9076146 5 5

Page 1 Explanation:
The illustrated tartan is the Royal Stewart. The motto on
the crest badge means 'Courage grows strong at a wound'.
The artist's montage depicts Holyroodhouse, with the
clan's plant badge, the Oak, in the foreground.

Stewart Country

The map used below and on the following page is intended basically as a pictorial reference. It is accurate enough, however, to be correlated with a current map. The clan boundaries are only marginally correct. No precise boundaries were kept in early times and territories were fluctuating frequently.

SEE DETAIL
MAP OVERLEAF

Stewart

CLAN MAP

1. Ardvorlich House Stronghold of Balquhidder Stewarts

2. Castle Stalker Stewart of Appin stronghold

3. Culloden Final defeat of Bonnie Prince Charlie

4. Darnaway Castle Northernmost seat

5. Doune Castle A seat of Moray branch

6. Dunkeld Cathedral Wolf of Badenoch believed buried here

7. Edinburgh Castle Held by Stewarts at times during stormy past

8. Falkland Palace A favourite seat of the Scottish Court

9. Glenfinnan Standard raised by Bonnie Prince Charlie, 1745

10. Linlithgow Palace Birthplace of Mary, Queen of Scots

11. Loch Leven Castle Mary, Queen of Scots held prisoner

12. Mount Stuart Palatial modern seat of Marquis of Bute

13. Palace of Holyroodhouse Rich in Stuart history

14. Rothesay Castle Stuart of Bute fortress

15. Stirling Castle Mary, Queen of Scots crowned here

16. Traquair House Picturesque early mansion with strong Stuart loyalty

The McIan illustration of Stewart as published (mid-19th century) in 'The Clans of the Scottish Highlands'

CLAN
STEWART

Condensed from Highland Clans of Scotland
George Eyre-Todd, 1923

When Shakespeare, in writing *Macbeth,* paid his great compliment to King James VI. and I., he was drawing attention to the popular tradition that the monarch's lineage was at least as far descended as that of the English nobility whose ancestors "came over with William the Conqueror." Whether the Stewarts were really descended from Banquo, Thane or Lochaber in the eleventh century, may be disputed, but there can be no question of their descent from Walter Fitz-Alan, the Shropshire knight whom David I. settled at Renfrew about the year 1138.

The purpose of that settlement is tolerably clear. The burning question of the hour for the Scottish monarch was the menace of Norse invasion in the Firth of Clyde. To oppose this invasion, David planted Walter Fitz-Alan where he could best bar the way to the heart of the kingdom, and made him Steward of Scotland. Most efficiently that guardian of the gate justified his appointment, driving the Norsemen out of Cowal and Bute, and when the mighty Somerled of the Isles brought an army to force the passage, overthrowing and slaying him at Renfrew itself in the year 1164. It was possibly as a thank-offering for this victory that Walter the Steward founded Paisley Abbey in that year.

For exactly another hundred years the great struggle went on, till in 1263, Walter's great-grandson, Alexander, now Lord High Steward of Scotland, finally overthrew the Norsemen under their king Hakon, at the battle of Largs.

Alexander's son James, who died in 1309, was the fifth High Steward or Stewart. From his brother, Sir John Stewart of Bonkyl, who fell fighting along with Wallace for the cause of Scottish independence at the battle of Falkirk in 1298, a number of famous Scottish families took their origin. The line of his eldest son, Sir Alexander, became Earls of Angus, and ended in a female who carried the earldom to the Douglases, who are Earls of Angus and Dukes of Hamilton at the present day. From his second son, Sir Alan Stewart of Darnley, descended the Stewart Earls of Lennox, whose heir, Lord Darnley married Mary Queen of Scots, and became ancestor of the later Stewart kings. From Sir Alan also descended the Earls of Galloway, who are chiefs of the Stewarts at the present hour. From Bonkyl's fourth son came the Stewarts of Innermeath in Strathearn, from who descended the Stewart Lords of Lorn, the Stewarts of Murthly and Grandtully, the Stewart Earls of Athol, and the Stewarts of Appin. And from Bonkyl's sixth son, Sir Robert, came the Stewarts of Allanton and their cadets.

Meantime, Bonkyl's nephew, Walter, the sixth High Stewart, had greatly distinguished himself in the cause of King Robert the Bruce, at the great battle of Bannockburn, and at the heroic defence of Berwick, and as a reward had received the hand of Bruce's only daughter, the Princess Marjory. Their married life was short. As she rode by the Knock between Renfrew and Paisley, Marjory was thrown from her horse and killed, and the life of her infant was only saved by the Cæsarean operation. The spot was long marked by the monolith known as Queen Bleary's Stone. The boy lived, however, and though he inherited his mother's weakness of the eyes, played a heroic part in Scottish history. From that old possession of his family, the island of Bute, which his ancestor had won from the Norsemen, he sallied forth to attack Dunoon and overthrow the entire conquest of Edward Baliol, and when he came to the throne as King Robert II. in 1371 He had earned it by his sword almost as heroically as his grandfather Robert the Bruce himself.

It is a point which has not been sufficiently noted by Scottish

Bannockburn

Falkland Palace

historians that from the two marriages of Robert II. a large proportion of the later troubles of the Stewart kings and of the kingdom of Scotland took rise. For centuries it was questioned whether his first union, with Elizabeth Mure of Rowallan, had ever been legitimised. In consequence the descendants of his second wife, Euphemia Ross, again and again made claim to the throne. From this cause arose directly the murder of King James I. in 1437 and the Douglas wars against James II. in 1450. James I. was slain by the descendants of King Robert's second wife, whom he had dispossessed of the royal earldom of Strathearn; and the ambition of the Earls of Douglas was directly stimulated by the fact that they had inherited the claims of the family of Euphemia Ross and of the earlier great house of Comyn.

Other of the troubles of Scotland arose from the family arrangements of King Robert II. in another way. One of his daughters, Margaret, he married to John, Lord of the Isles, and as John was already married to his cousin Amy, he made him put her away, granted him a charter of her lands, and made the title and great possessions of the Lord of the Isles to descend to his own grandchildren, Margaret's sons. From this arrangement came endless trouble. Not even yet has it been settled absolutely whether Glengarry or Clanranald, the descendants of John's first wife, or Macdonald of the Isles, the descendant of his second wife, is the rightful Chief of the Macdonalds. From the first also there was trouble among the sons and grandsons of Robert II. His eldest son, King Robert III., whose real name was John, was practically displaced by his brother Robert, Duke of Albany, who first starved the king's eldest son to death at Falkland, and then secured the capture and imprisonment of the second son in England. And by way of reprisals, when he returned from his captivity, that second son, James I., sent to the block the Duke's son and grandsons who had succeeded to Albany's usurpation. Meanwhile the north of Scotland had been laid waste by the wars between the Duke of Albany and his sister's son, Donald of the Isles, for possession of the rich Earldom of Ross — wars which only came to an end with the terrific and bloody battle of Harlaw, fought near Aberdeen in 1411.

The leaders in that conflict were Donald of the Isles himself and his cousin Alexander Stewart, Earl of Mar. The latter had obtained his earldom by slaying the husband of Isabel, Countess of Mar, and

14

Glen Sannox, Isle of Bute

then marrying the lady. He was a natural son of the fierce "Wolf of Badenoch," Alexander Stewart, Earl of Buchan, third son of King Robert II., who is remembered solely by his lawless deeds in the north, the burning of Forres and Elgin, and countless other oppressions. He had many illegitimate children, and many of the name of Stewart in Atholl and Banffshire are his descendants.

A notable Stewart family in the south, that of Bute, is directly descended from Robert II. himself. On succeeding to the throne, that king appointed his natural son, John Stewart of Dundonald, known as the Red Stewart, to be Constable of Rothesay Castle and Hereditary Sheriff of Bute, thus handing to his son and that son's descendants in perpetuity the islands which had been captured by the sword of his ancestor, Walter Fitz-Alan, the first of the Stewarts. After the execution of Murdoch, Duke of Albany, and two of his sons at the instance of James I. in 1425, a third son who had escaped took vengeance by burning Dunbarton, and in it this same Red Stewart of Dundonald, uncle of the king. But Sir John Stewart's direct descendant is Marquess of Bute at the present hour.

Two of the sons of Murdoch, Duke of Albany, also left natural sons. Of them, Walter Stewart of Morphy, son of Sir Walter Stewart, beheaded at Stirling, became ancestor of the Earls of Castle-Stuart in Ireland, and also, by the marriage of a descendant to the daughter of the Regent Earl of Moray, half-brother of Mary Queen of Scots, became ancestor of the Earls of Moray of to-day. Another of Duke Murdoch's sons, Sir James Mohr Stewart, had a natural son, James "beg" Stewart of Baldorran, who became ancestor of the Stewarts of Ardvorlich on Lochearnside, whose family history is recounted by Sir Walter Scott is *A Legend of Montrose*.

Most romantic of all the memories of the Stewarts, however, is probably that connected with the settlement of the race in Lorn, Appin, and Atholl. On the death of Ewen, Lord of Lorn, of the days of Robert II., his estates passed to his daughters and co-heiresses. These daughters had married two brothers, John and Robert Stewart of Innermeath, descendants of the fourth son of Sir John Stewart of Bonkyl, already referred to. These two brothers made a bargain. Robert gave up his wife's share of Lorn in exchange for his brother's share of Innermeath. Sir John Stewart who thus relinquished his share of Innermeath and became Lord of all Lorn, had a second son Sir James, known as the Black Knight of Lorn. After the assassination of James I. at the Charterhouse of Perth in 1437, this Black Knight married the widowed Queen Joan, and they had a son, John, who was of course half-brother to the king, James II. When that king in 1450 finally overthrew the last Earl of Douglas, he found a fair lady on his hands. This lady, known from her beauty as the Fair Maid of Galloway, was the heiress to all the great Douglas estates, and, as a child, had been married in succession by William, Earl of Douglas, whom James stabbed in Stirling Castle, and his brother, Earl James, who was overthrown at Arkinhilme. While Earl James fled into exile in England, from which he was only to return to die a monk at Lindores, the king procured a divorce for his fair young wife, and married her to his own half-brother, John, son of Queen Joan and the Black Knight of Lorn. He conferred upon the pair the Douglas lordship of Balveny, and they became presently Earl and Countess of Atholl. The Earl played a distinguished part in three reigns. On the death of the fifth Stewart Earl of Atholl, in 1595, the title passed first to Stewart of Innermeath, and afterwards, on the Innermeath line becoming extinct, to John Murray, son of the eldest daughter of the fifth Earl, by his marriage with the second Earl of Tullibardine. The direct descendant of that union is Duke of Atholl at the present day.

Meanwhile through Robert, elder brother of the Black Knight of Lorn, the line of the Stewart Lords of Lorn was carried on. The line ended in two heiresses who married Campbells, when this family secured the Lordship of Lorn. A natural son of Stewart of Lorn, however, with the help of his mother's people, the Clan MacLaurin, succeeded in seizing and retaining the district of Appin and founding the family of the Stewarts of Appin. In the days of James IV., Duncan Stewart of Appin built on an islet in Loch Linnhe the stronghold of Castle Stalker in which he entertained his "cousin" the King. During the Jacobite rising in 1745 under prince Charles Edward the Appin Stewarts, led by Stewart of Ardsheal, played a conspicuous part. Sir Walter Scott in *Waverley* tells how Stewart of Invernahyle saved the life of Colonel Whiteford of Ballochmyle, and how, after the overthrow at Culloden, Colonel Whiteford returned the obligation by obtaining a pardon for Invernahyle by a special and chivalrous interview at

Stirling Castle

Whitehall. In Appin itself a cave is shown behind a waterfall, in which Ardsheal hid for a time from the red soldiers, as well as the hollow in the top of a great boulder in which he was afterwards concealed. As a result the Appin estates were forfeited for a time, and while they were under the management of Campbell of Glenure the famous Appin murder took place which forms the pivot of R. L. Stevenson's famous story *Kidnapped*. The spot where Glenure was shot is marked by a cairn behind Kentalen. The supposed murderer was Alan Breck Stewart, who escaped to France, but as a victim James Stewart of the Glens was seized, tried by the Campbells at Inveraray, and hanged in chains on the little mount behind Ballachulish Hotel.

From Alexander, younger brother of the Black Knight of Lorn, are descended the Stewarts of Grandtully below Aberfeldy in Perthshire. It was Sir James Stewart of Grandtully who, before he succeeded to the family title and estates, ran away with Lady Jane, sister of the first and last Duke of Douglas, and whose son by her was the claimant in the great Douglas Cause. The House of Lords declared Archibald Stewart to be really Lady Jane's son, and he accordingly came into possession of the great Douglas estates, and was created Lord Douglas by George III.

Of the main line of the Stewarts, as represented by the kings of that name, the history is too well known to need recounting her. Of two of its members, Mary Queen of Scots and Bonnie Prince Charlie, the careers are among the most romantic and moving in the world's annals. From first to last these Stewart kings were consistently unfortunate, yet their lives give a brilliance and glamour to history that is entirely lacking from the sedate annals of other dynasties. Their legitimate male line came to an end with Henry, Cardinal York, the younger brother of Prince Charles, who died in 1807, but three of the great ducal houses of the country, those of Buccleuch, Richmond and Gordon, and St. Albans, are directly descended from natural sons of King Charles II.

The spelling of the name Stuart, used by the royal family and the Marquess of Bute was probably introduced by Queen Mary on her return from France.

Mary, Queen of Scots

Inner Court of the Palace of Linlithgow

Stuart, Mary, Queen of Scots, daughter of James V. and Mary of Guise, was born in the palace of Linlithgow, December 7, 1542. Her father was on his death-bed when her birth was announced and seven days after that event he expired.

The young queen was crowned on the 9th of September, 1543, while she was only nine months old. In her sixth year she was sent to France, to receive the refined education which that country then, above all others, was capable of affording.

A desire long entertained by Mary's mother and Henry of France to unite the interests of the two kingdoms, had early produced a contract of marriage between Francis, the young dauphin, and the Scottish queen, and the youthful pair were accordingly united. Mary was then in the sixteenth year of her age, and her husband but little older. Already Queen of Scotland and heir-presumptive of England, Mary was now, by her marriage to the dauphin, queen-consort apparent of France. The last of these honours was realized, but only for a short period. In 1559, a year after her marriage, her husband succeeded to the throne by the death of his father; but in another year afterwards, in 1560, he died, while yet only in the seventeenth year of his age. On the death of her husband Mary was invited to return to Scotland, in order to undertake the government. Her reception in her native land was warm and enthusiastic.

The long series of miseries and misfortunes, which render her history so remarkable, began with her unfortunate marriage to Darnley on the 29th of July, 1565.

Henry Stuart, Lord Darnley, at the time of his marriage was in the nineteenth year of his age; Mary in her twenty-third. Darnley was esteemed one of the handsomest men of his time; but, unfortunately, he was weak, obstinate, and wayward.

Amongst the first evil results which this unfortunate connection produced to Mary, was the hostility of her brother the Earl of Murray, who foresaw that the new king-consort would greatly lessen the power and influence which he enjoyed whilst his sister remained single. Seventeen days after the celebration of the queen's marriage, Murray, who now stood forward as an open and decl ared enemy, summoned his partisans to meet him, armed, at Ayr. Being finally driven to Carlisle, whither he was followed by Mary with an army now increased to 18,000 men, his troops there dispersed, and he fled to the English court.

This triumph of Mary's, however, in place of securing her the quiet which might have been expected seemed merely to have opened a way for the admission of other miseries. Murray and the other lords now endeavoured to secure, by plot and contrivance, that which they had failed to obtain by force. They found a ready co-operator in the Earl of Morton, who was now amongst the few counsellors whom Mary had left. Working on the vanity and weakness of Darnley, Morton succeeded in inducing him to join a conspiracy, which had for its object the restoration of the banished lords and the wresting from, or putting under restraints, the authority of the queen. There was, however, one person whose fidelity to the queen made him sufficiently dangerous to render it necessary that he should be removed. This was David Rizzio, Mary's secretary. On the 9th of March, 1565, the conspirators entered the queen's chamber while she was at supper with several of her household. Rizzio was dragged into an adjoining apartment, and despatched with no fewer than fifty-six wounds.

At this critical period the vacilating Darnley, allowed himself to be persuaded by Mary, to assist and accompany her in making her escape from Holyrood.

Mary and her husband left the palace for Dunbar. Here the queen found herself, in the course of a few days, surrounded by half of her nobility, and at the head of a powerful army. With these she returned, after an absence of only five days, in triumph to Edinburgh, where she was again reinstated in full and uncontrolled authority.

Soon after the occurrence of the events just related Mary was delivered of a son, afterwards James VI. of Scotland and I. of England. From this period the page of Mary's history rapidly darkens.

At the suggestion of the Earl of Bothwell the privy-council submitted to Mary the proposal that she should divorce Darnley. It was the first step of the new ambition of Bothwell, which aimed at the hand of his sovereign. Mary refused to accede to the proposal. This resolution, however, in place of diverting Bothwell had the effect only of driving him to a more desperate expedient. He now resolved that Darnley should die. Attended by a band of accomplices, he proceeded, at midnight on Sunday the 9th of February, 1567, to the

Murder of David Rizzio

Kirk of Field House, where Darnley, who was at the time unwell, had taken up a temporary residence. In a few minutes the house, with all its inmates, including Darnley, was totally destroyed.

Suspicion at length became so strong against the perpetrator, that, at the instigation of Darnley's father, the Earl of Lennox, he was brought to trial. Bothwell, however, was too powerful a man to fear the result. On the day of trial no one appeared to prosecute him, and he was acquitted. Bothwell procured the signatures of a number of the nobility to a document setting forth, first, his innocence of that crime; secondly, the necessity of the queen's entering again into the married state; and lastly, recommending James, Earl of Bothwell as fit to become her husband. In two or three days after this Mary left Edinburgh for Stirling, and as she was returning she was waylaid by Bothwell.

Bothwell, having dismissed all her attendants, seized the bridle of Mary's horse, and immediately the whole cavalcade proceeded to Dunbar, one of Bothwell's castles. Here Mary was detained for ten days, during which Bothwell had succeeded in obtaining her consent to espouse him. The queen and her future husband returned to Edinburgh and a few weeks afterwards were married. Bothwell, however, did not long enjoy the success of his villany. A number of those very lords who had assisted him together with many others, took up arms to displace him. Bothwell hastily collected at Dunbar a force of 2000 men, and with these marched towards Edinburgh. Negotiations were entered into, and the final result of these was, that Mary, who had accompanied Bothwell to the field, offered to deliver herself up to the opposite party, on condition that they would conduct her safely to Edinburgh, and thereafter yield to her authority.

Mary's captors for they now stood in that position, conveyed her eventually to Holyrood, and on to the castle of Lochleven, situated on a small island in a lake of that name in Fifeshire.

On the 24th of July, 1567, Lord Lindsay and Sir Robert Lindsay, deputed by the lords of secret council, proceeded to Lochleven, and by threats compelled Mary to sign a deed of abdication, a proceeding which was soon after followed by the election of Murray to the regency. Bothwell, in the meantime, after some ineffectual attempts to regain his lost authority, embarked for Denmark. He attempted, on his way thither, to replenish his exhausted finances by piracy. On his landing he was thrown into prison, where he remained for many years, and finally ended his days in misery and neglect.

Though Mary's fortunes were at this low ebb, and her enemies numerous and powerful, she had still many friends, who waited anxiously for an opportunity of asserting her rights; and for such an opportunity, although it was unsuccessful, they had not to wait long. The attempt was made under the auspices of William Douglas, a young man of sixteen years of age. Douglas, having purloined the keys of the fortress, liberated the captive princess and conveyed her to the shore. Here she was met, with joy and loyal affection by a number of her nobility. In a few days Mary found herself at the head of a formidable army. She now solemnly and publicly protested that her abdication had been compulsory, and therefore not valid, and called upon Murray to surrender his regency. This he refused to do, and both parties prepared for hostilities. On Thursday the 13th of May, 1568, Murray, who was at Glasgow, having learned that the queen with her forces were on their way to Dumbarton hastily assembled an army and marched to Langside to intercept her. A battle followed, fatal to the hopes of Mary. Resolving at length to throw herself on the protection of Elizabeth, she embarked on board a fishing boat, and, sailing along the shore until she arrived at Workington in Cumberland, was there landed with her suite. From Workington she proceeded to Cockermouth, where she was conducted with every mark of respect to the castle of Carlisle. This honourable treatment, however, was of short duration. Mary was now in the hands of her bitterest and most inveterate enemy, Elizabeth.

On the 25th of September, 1586, Mary was removed to the Castle of Fotheringay, with a view to her being brought to trial on a charge of having abetted a conspiracy which had for its object the assassination of Elizabeth and the liberation of the captive queen. The trial was adjourned to the Star Chamber at Westminster, where Elizabeth's parliament alleged that their sovereign's security was incompatible with Mary's life, and urged her to order her immediate execution.

Mary's remains were embalmed and buried in the cathedral at Peterborough, but twenty-five years afterwards were removed by her son James VI. to Westminster Abbey. She was at the time of her death in the forty-fifth year of her age, and the nineteenth of her captivity.

Bonnie Prince Charlie

Bonnie Prince Charlie

Condensation of Victorian article

In song and story has the stirring narrative of the exploits of Bonnie Prince Charlie come to us, and for a man to land in a populous island like ours, with only seven followers, and to hope to win a kingdom, is a fitting theme for a weaver of romance. Yet that is what Charles Edward Stuart did in 1745 at Glenaladale, in Moidart after the French army of 12,000 men which set out to help him was wrecked and all the troops had perished. Practically all the West Highland chiefs amongst whom he landed were against the rising in view of the small means the Prince then had at his disposal, but, despite their fears, all the important ones save two joined him.

These marched to Edinburgh and the Prince was received with wild enthusiasm. His army swelled to 2,400 men, but, owing to the recent Disarming Act, many were armed only with scythes, and pitchforks. None the less, all were eager to meet General Cope, who with 3,000 foot and horse and six guns, had taken up a strong position between Prestonpans and the coaling village of Tranent. Cope had all the advantages of the dykes and enclosures and was protected by a morass, while many of his troops were veterans. The Highlanders kept to the high ground and during the night a gentleman of the neighbourhood named Anderson led them down through the morass to the plain on which the Hanoverian troops lay.

The attack was made with terrific swiftness; the Camerons and Stewarts stormed the battery, and then drove Gardiner's Dragoons before them like sheep. The Macdonalds dashed upon Hamilton's Dragoons and put them to flight. The Highland centre charged the famed Royal Infantry of England and in five minutes had broken the bayonets as they did later at Culloden, and Cope's whole army was a wreck. The infantry, who had behaved bravely, suffered most, but the Highlanders were quick to give quarter, and the Prince did his utmost to "save his father's subjects", as he put it.

Next day Prince Charlie's army entered Edinburgh in triumph. With 6,000 men he marched on Carlisle and took the city, and then went on as far as Derby. The generalship had been excellent so far and Charles was all in favour of marching straight to London. The Prince's advisers, however, thought otherwise, and so the fatal blunder of retreat was committed. They had evaded two armies by their brilliant tactics, and so had placed themselves between the King's troops, 24,000 men, and London. Help was promised from France, from the Welsh Jacobites, and from those in London. Charles was furious, but his expostulations were in vain, and in a spirit of utter disgust the clansmen, who had hoped to see London and always hated retreat, retraced their steps northwards. They scored a brillian rearguard victory at Shap, which checked Cumerland's army. Charles also besieged Stirling Castle, and at Falkirk won a complete victory over General Hawley who owned to having 2,000 more men than the Prince.

The rest of the Prince's history is a record of disaster from the moment of the neglect of Lord John Drummond, who should have held the passage of the river Spey against Cumberland, to the defeat of the exhausted Highlanders at Culloden. Quarrels divided the little army and contributed in no small degree to its defeat. From that time (April, 1746) to September, the Prince wandered, a homeless fugitive, amongst the Highland people of the West. Poor as they were, they spurned the huge reward offered by the Government for the Prince dead or alive. Thanks to them and to help from Lady MacDonald of Sleat and MacDonald of Milton, who sent his famous sister Flora to be his guide in one of his most dangerous moments, the Prince was able to escape to France.

Culloden

Some Clan Notables

Stuart, Alexander *(1673-1742)* Possibly born in Aberdeen this notable physiologist graduated from Marischal College, Aberdeen. At Cambridge he distinguished himself with his innovative and amazingly accurate hypotheses concerning the behaviour of muscles in the human body.

Stewart, William *(1769-1854)* A grandson of Donald Stewart of Appin, one of Bonnie Prince Charlie's officers, he was sent to New South Wales as the senior military officer. He was appointed lieutenant governor under Darling who regarded him highly and made him a member of the Land Board.

Stewart, Andrew *(1789-1822)* This Glaswegian entered the service of the Hudson's Bay Company in 1811 as a writer at Moose Factory. In 1814-15 he was the master there. He was promoted to the rank of chief trader.

Stuart, John *(1815-1866)* This versatile native of Fife, Scotland was an engineer, surveyor and explorer in Central Australia where he is commemorated by Mount Stuart. He was the first to discover an all-season, north-south route across Australia's interior.

Stewart, James *(1832-1914)* A Perthshire native who emigrated to New Zealand as a civil engineer where he soon began a remarkable career. A special interest was the railway where he played a vital role in the newly developing network.

Stewart, George *(1860-1930)* A medical scientist raised in Scotland whose investigations concerned the velocity of blood flow, temperature regulation and the cardiac nerves. He came to America in 1893 as an instructor at Harvard and was head of the department of physiology at the University of Chicago, 1903-7. In 1910-15 he devised and applied the calorimtric method of measuring blood flow suitable for clinical use.

Stewart Associated Names

Associated names have a hazy history. Sometimes they had more than one origin; also clouding the precise location of a particular surname might be that name's proscription or of course a migrant population. Even the spelling of surnames was subject to great variations, shifting from usually Latin or Gaelic and heeding rarely to consistent spelling. In early records there can be several spellings of the same name. Undoubtedly contributing to this inconsistency is the handwriting in official records, which was often open to more than one spelling interpretation.

With regard to the 'Mac' prefix, this was, of course, from the Gaelic meaning, son of. It wasn't long before it was abbreviated to 'Mc' or 'M', until we have reached the position now where there are more 'Mc's' than 'Mac's'.

BANNATYNE From unknown nameplace. Some of the Bannatynes of Bute were followers of Stewarts of Bute. Nicol de Benauty in 1303 vice regent of earl of Carrick. Bannatyne and Ballantyne used interchangeably, even within family, for a long period. The laird of Kames, chief of the Bannatynes or MacCamelynes rendered homage to Stewart of Bute in 1547.

BOYD Possibly derivative from island of Bute. Gaelic for marquess of Bute is Morair Bhoid. First recorded Boyds in Largs. Dommus Robertus de Boyd, miles, contract witness in 1205, Irvine. Walterus de Boht witnessed gift to monastery of Paisley, about 1272.

CARMICHAEL, MACMICHAEL The Stewarts of Galloway and Appin both possibly involved with this name. The Carmichaels moved from Galloway to Appin. In Lanarkshire there is a parish of this name. Robert de Carmitely, about 1220, resigned all patronage claims to church of Cleghorn. Sir John de Carmychell obtained land charter for 'Carmychell' lands between 1374-84. William de Carmychale, charter witness in St. Andrews, 1410.

COMBE Like an abbreviation for MacComb. Payment was recorded being made to Robert Comb of Edinburgh, 1728. Two brothers were notable: George Combe, phrenologist (1788-1858) and brother Andrew, physician (1797-1847).

CRUICKSHANK, CRUISKSHANKS, CRUIKSHANK Unlikely to refer to crooked shanks, this Stewart sept has close connections with Kincardine and Aberdeen. It may well be that the river Cruick joining the North Esk in Kincardine and the shank, projecting point of hill, may well have accounted for name. John Crokeshanks, Haddington burgess, 1296. Cristinus Cru(k)sank, Aberdeen burgess, 1408. Adam Crukshank served as vicar of Cruden, 1414.

FULLERTON From nameplace, Fullarton in Dundonald, Ayrshire. Alanus de Fowlertoun founded a covenant at Irvine in 13th century. A son had charters to lands in Kyle, Ayrshire. Believed a branch of this family moved to Arran, where given charter to lands in Kilmichael, Bute and became a Stewart of Bute sept.

GLASS From Gaelic adjective glas, grey or abbreviated form of MacGille glais, son of the grey lad. Stewart association through Glass of Ascog in Bute, 15th century. In 1506 Alexander Glass granted lands on Bute. The name also occurs in Perth, 1674. Donald Glass, Dingwall resident, 1652.

GRAY Possibly from Gray, a French town and also from Anglicizing MacGlashan, a Stewart of Ballechin sept. Hugo de Gray witnessed a charter by Walter de Lundin, about 1248. William de Grey witnessed resignation of lands of Nysebyte, 1255. William Gray charter witness at Newton of Ayr, about 1280.

HUNTER From the chase. In Latin, venator. Occurs in many parts of Scotland early, hence little chance of common ancestor. William venator, Inquisition witness, before 1124. Yone Venatore Beauly charter witness, 1231. Aymon Hunter, bailie of Cullen, 1328.

JAMIESON From son of James. Stewart association through family called Jamieson or Nelson, who were Crowners of Bute from 14th century or earlier to 17th century. William Jamyson, Coupar Angus tenant, 1472. John Jamyson, Aberdeen burgess, 1465.

LENNOX A place name derived from one of the Stewart titles. In 1400 John of Levenx, the Duke of Albany's man, was safely conducted into England. In 1428 John de Lenox, witness to Glasgow tenement sale. Walter Lennox recorded in parish of Campsie, 1669.

LIVINGSTON, LIVINGSTONE From nameplace in West Lothian and also associated with Appin Stewarts. From Gaelic, Mac-an-Leigh is MacLay, an Appin sept, and Livingston. In 1296 Sir Archibald de Levingstoune of Edinburgh rendered homage. James de Leyffingstoun, in 1496, great chamberlain of Scotland. Explorer David Livingstone, from MacLeays of Appin background.

MACCOLL From Gaelic MacColla, son of Coll. Followers of Stewart of Appin. In 1720, Mathew M'Koll, a merchant burgess of Edinburgh was paid £25. In the rebellion of 1745, eighteen Maccols were killed in the Stewart of Appin regiment.

MACGLASHAN Originated from Gaelic M'Glaisein, a diminutive of M'Ghille ghlais, son of the grey lad. Formerly of the Stewart of Ballechin family but renounced name after family disagreement and changed to MacGlashan. Iain McGalssan or McGlassane massacred at Dunavertie, 1647. David McKglashen was recorded as 'Saboth braker' in Croy, 1681.

MACKINLAY, MACKINLEY Originates from Gaelic form of Finlayson. Although a Scots name, also occurs in Antrim, Ulster from Scots who settled there. Commonly found in Glelyon and Balquhidder. Gillaspyk M'Kinlay acted as witness, Craignish, 1493. Donald M'Kindlay recorded in Innerchocheill, Dunkeld, 1696.

MACKIRDY, MACMURTIE, MACKIRDY Common in Arran and Bute. Sir James M'Wartye recorded as vicar of Kingarth, Bute, 1554. James Makilvertie is form of MacKirdie. First showing in Ayrshire, Lanarkshire. Gilbert Mamurtyre, Edinburgh witness, 1508. William M'Mowtrie, Edinburgh soldier, 1684.

MACMICHAEL From Gaelic MacMicheil, son of the servant of St. Michael. MacGill-Mhichell, common in Bute, late 18th century. Gillecolme Makgillemichael, charter witness, Lismore, Argyllshire, 1251. John Makmuchell, Prestwick burgess, 1507.

MITCHELL Originated with Hebrew name Michael, softened by French form Michel. French influence likely in Scots origin of name. In 1489 John Michell granted remission for his part in holding Dumbarton Castle against the King. John Mitsell, Glasgow landowner, 1496. Mitchell M'Brair, Galloway resident, 1490.

MITCHELSON Meaning is son of Michael. Common in Newburgh, Fife in mid-16 th century Michelson. Latin genetive used in early records of name. In 1398 John Michelsone had safe conduct into England. In 1435 Donald Michaelis was serving as vicar of Lethnot. In Glasgow, Henry Michallis is recorded as a notary, 1454.

MONTEITH Originates from nameplace in Perthshire. In 1237 Malcolm de Manetheth appears as witness. Colin de Mentaghe served as juror on inquisition, Perth, 1305. In 1496 Thomas Mentheith is recorded as Glaswegian landholder.

MOODIE, MOODY Possibly from old English, modig, courageous. Johannes Modi served on Peebles' inquest. Merchant William Mudy had safe conduct into England, 1365. Burial place for Mudies erected in Dundee, 1602.

MUNN From MacMunn, is Gaelic meaning son of the servant of St Munn. Sir John Munn, procurator-fiscal of vicar's of choir of Glasgow, 1551. Catherine Munn, born Tobermory, Mull (died 1860) composed song, 'O, my love is for the laddie'.

NIELSON Two Scots origins for this name, son of Neil. The Nielsons of Craigcaffie, Stranraer, Ayrshire, trace descent from Neil, earl of Carrick, husband of Margaret Stewart, who died, 1256. They added 'son' to Neil. John Nielsoun, Glasgow baker, 1554. The other origin for name occurred in Caithness where Nelesoun granted lands in 1429.

ROBB Diminutive form of Robert. Jack Robb, a registered voter in Monkland, 1519. Nicholas Rob was Dumfriesshire witness, 1542. Down payment for land in Logie, Stirlingshire made by Janet Rob, 1563.

SHARP Possibly from old Gaelic name Macilheran, which was Anglicized to Sharp. William Scharp, tenant of earl of Douglas in Broughton, 1376. Patrick Sharp, landholder, Aberdeen, 1439. John Scharpe, Dumfries merchant, 1656.

WALKER From Middle English, walker, a thickener of woollen cloth, and Latin fullo. Highland rendering of Walker is Gaelic Mac an fhucadair. In 1324 Thomas dictus Walker recorded in Berwick. Andrew and John fulloni were Douglas tenants in Buittle, Kirkcudbrightshire, 1376. Donald Walcare, landowner, Edinburgh, 1457.